This book has been percolating in my head for a couple of years and I have tried many approaches to figuring out an easy way to construct these Circles of Life. The beads are meant to represent important events in your life such as birthdays, holidays, anniversaries and weddings. I have enjoyed thinking up additional beads to compliment the ones I started with.

The book also contains instructions for several beaded charms to hang from charm spacers. I could have included several more charms but at some point I told myself to stop and get on with the basics. Of course if you wish you could purchase some ready made charms to represent other events in your life such as graduation or cancer awareness charms.

I would like to thank my husband, Chuck Cancelliere, for allowing me the opportunity to bead, bead, bead while he takes care of the day to day things in life. Were it not for his complete support, this book would have taken much longer to produce.

I want to thank all my pattern testers – Darla Deaton, Pam Hunt and Karie Hieb - for their diligence in testing these designs and giving me comments that would make things easier for you to follow.

Finally I would like to thank my daughter, Chelsea Townes, for her graphic art work on this production. Were it not for her, as graphically challenged as I am, this book would not exist. Although I draw out the diagrams, she makes them more pleasant to look at than my original drawings and takes care of the page layout. The very talented Rebecca Philpot is the photographer for all of the photos in this book.

Table of Contents

Basic Beading Materials and Supplies 6
Constructing the Base 7
Circles of Life
    Birthstone Petal Circle 8
    Birthstone Braided Circle 9
    Birthstone Cubes and Pearls Circle 10
    Flower Box Circle 11
    Gemstone and Pearl Circle 12
    Anniversary Circle 14
    Double Anniversary Circle 15
    Small Hearts Circle 16
    Crystal Net Circle 22
    Netted Overlay Circle 24
Spacer Beads
    Single Rope Spacer 17
    Crystal Rope Spacer 18
    Double Rope Spacer 19
    Seed Bead Embellished Spacer 20
    Charm Spacer 26
        Charms– heart 28
        Charms– Starfish 34
Twisted Herringbone Rope Necklace 39
Resources 40

Basic Beading Materials and Supplies

Beads
The beads used in the *Circles of Life* can be anything that you select as long as you stay close to the sizes for each circle. This is a great opportunity to rummage through your bead stash and pick out some special beads that have been waiting for the right idea.

Crystals
These designs use Swarovski crystals in 2mm round, 2.5mm bicone and 4mm round sizes. You can substitute any crystal or firepolish bead in the same sizes.

Seed Beads
The designs all begin with 15° round beads in a galvanized finish. Some of the designs use some 11° beads of a matching color.

Gemstones
Some of the designs use flat faceted gemstones. The size is about 5 to 6mm.

Pearls
Freshwater pearls 2 to 4mm sizes.

Thread and Needles
The designs in this book were stitched using 4 lb test Fireline. If your tension is very tight, you may want to switch to something stronger like Wildfire. Needles can be an 11 or 12, but for some gemstones you may need to move to a size 13 because they are likely to have smaller holes.

The embellishment and the repeated passes through the beads results in a firm circle. If your circles are not firm because your beading tension is too loose, you can dip the piece in Future Floor Wax, drain off the excess and let it dry. You may want to place it on a round object to maintain its shape as it dries. In general, though, the repeated passes through the beads will tighten it up.

Constructing the Base

The base

For most of the Circles of Life begins with placing 32 size 15° beads on fireline and tying into a circle leaving a tail that is long enough to weave in later. Work in tubular peyote for the required number of rows (depending on the width required for each style). The 32 original beads will be rows one and two so the first actual row that you peyote will be row three.

You need to remember to "step up" at the end of each round. This means after you add the last bead in each round you need to pass your needle through the first bead you added in that round so that your thread is coming out of an "up" bead. A diagram of the "step up" can be found on page 40.

The width of the base will vary depending on the finished design of the circles- it can be 5, 7 or even 11 rows.

You should end up with a cigar band shape for the base of the bead.

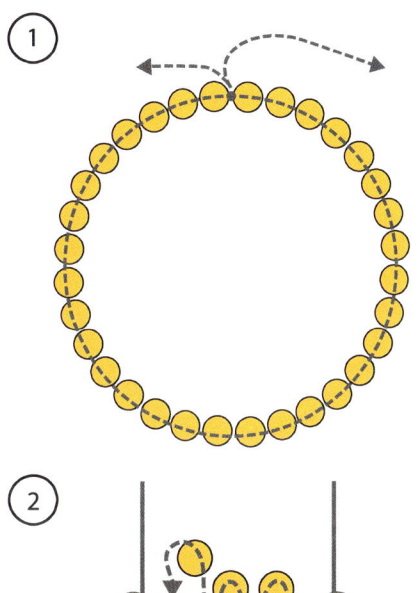

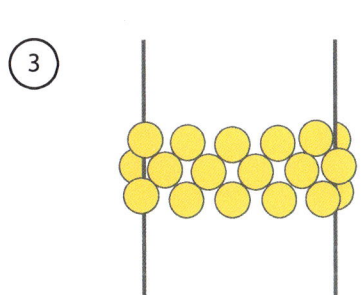

Birthstone Petal Circle

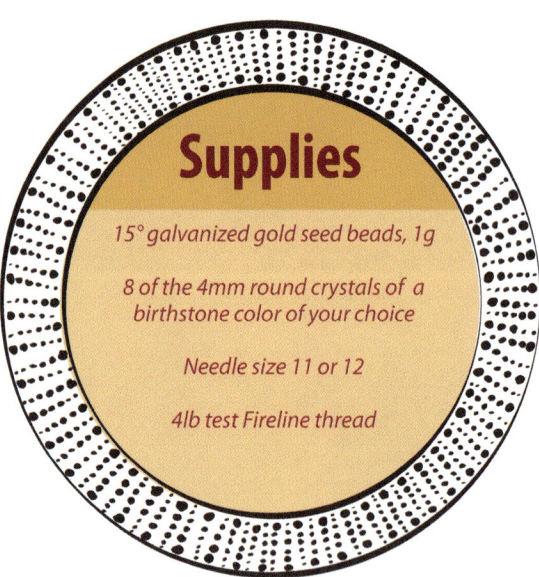

Supplies

15° galvanized gold seed beads, 1g

8 of the 4mm round crystals of a birthstone color of your choice

Needle size 11 or 12

4lb test Fireline thread

Instructions

Make a 5 row peyote base. Weave your needle to the middle bead in one of the stacks of three. String on one 15°, one 4mm round crystal, one 15° seed bead. Skip the next middle bead and go through the second middle bead.

Repeat until you have eight crystals on the base. Once the crystals are in place, embellishment helps to lock them in.

Weave your thread to the edge of the circle and come out one of the "up" beads that is in between the crystals. String on four 15° seed beads and go back through the fourth bead and the "up" bead in the opposite direction. You are forming a little picot in between the Crystals on the side of the wheel. Make sure that you go through the up bead in the opposite direction when you go back through it.

When you have completed all the picots on one side, weave the thread so that it is coming out of one of the "up" beads that is beside the crystal. String on two 15° beads and go through the top three beads of the picot made in the previous round. String on two more 15° beads and go through the "up" bead that is beside the next crystal. Continue around the circle.

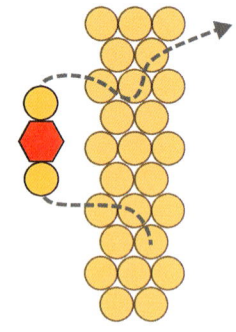

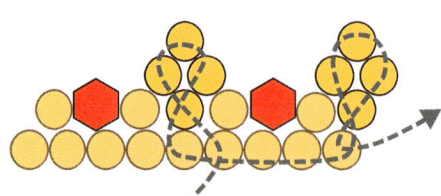

Repeat on the other side of the circle to embellish in the same way. After completing the second side, weave to the top of a picot and stitch the two picots together with a square stitch. Repeat the square stitch to reinforce. Weave through the beads to get to the next picot. Continue around the Circle. Tie off and bury the threads.

Birthstone Braided Circle

Supplies

15° galvanized gold seed beads, 1g

8 of the 4mm round crystals of a birthstone color of your choice

Needle size 11 or 12

4lb test Fireline thread

Instructions

Make a 5 row peyote base. Weave your needle to the middle bead in one of the stacks of three. String on one 15°, one 4mm round crystal, one 15° seed bead. Skip the next middle bead and go through the second middle bead.

Repeat until you have eight crystals on the wheel. Once the crystals are in place, embellishment helps to lock them in.

For the braided embellishment begin with the thread exiting the 15° "up" bead along the edge of the circle next to one of the crystals. String on 7 size 15° beads and go through the "up" bead on the opposite edge of the base that is in the center of the next crystal. Proceed around the entire circle on this aide adding 7 more loops of 7 beads. Pass the needle through the 1st 4 beads of the first loop. Pick up 3 seed beads and cross over to the other side of the base and go through the up bead of the next crystal. Repeat on the other side so that you are making an X. String on three beads use the center bead from the first side and then string on three more beads to complete the X.

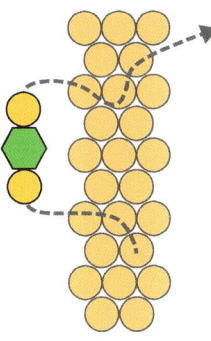

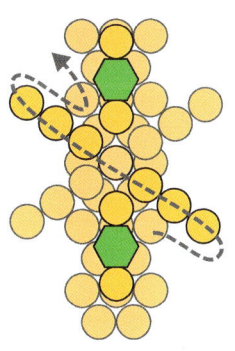

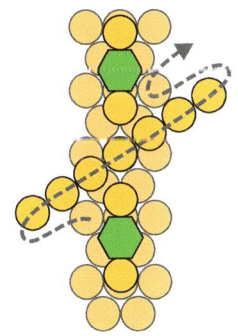

Birthstone Cubes and Pearls Circle

Supplies

15° galvanized gold seed beads, 1g

4 of the 4mm crystal cubes

4 of the 2 to 3 mm freshwater pearls

Needle size 11 or 12

4lb test Fireline thread

Instructions

Make a 5 row peyote base. Weave your needle to the middle bead in one of the stacks of three. String on two 15°, one 4mm cube crystal, two 15° seed bead. Skip the next middle bead and go through the second middle bead. Then string on one 15°, one pearl, one 15° and go through the second middle bead. Repeat around until you have four cubes and four pearls.

To embellish the sides use a 5 bead picot by exiting one of the "up" beads on one side of the circle. Pick up five 15° beads and go through the next "up" bead on that side. Repeat on the second side. Then connect the third bead of each picot together on the top of the circle. Using square stitch. Tie off and bury the threads.

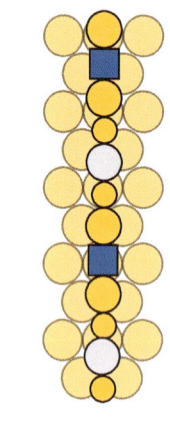
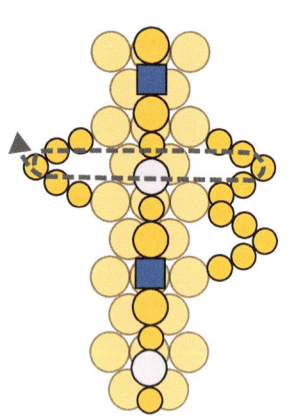
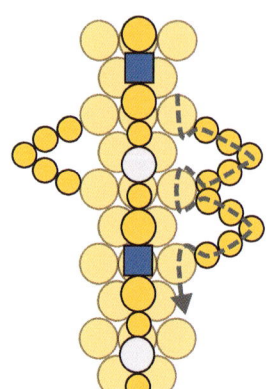

Flower Box Circle

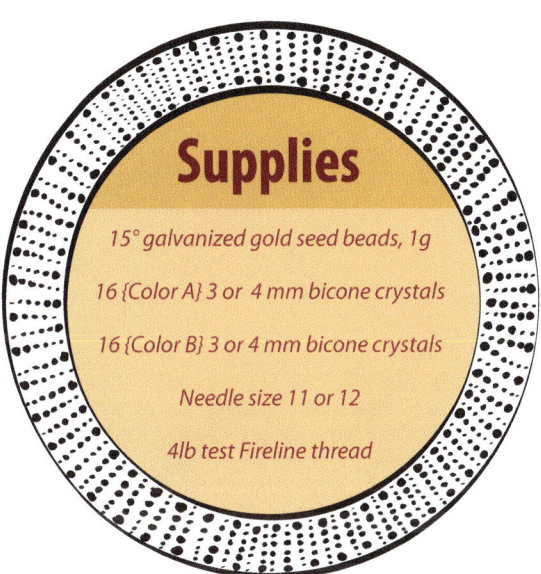

Supplies

15° galvanized gold seed beads, 1g

16 {Color A} 3 or 4 mm bicone crystals

16 {Color B} 3 or 4 mm bicone crystals

Needle size 11 or 12

4lb test Fireline thread

Instructions

Make a 5 row peyote base. The flowers are made with a cluster of four 3 or 4mm bicone crystals. With the thread exiting an "up" bead on the edge of the base, string on one crystal in {Color A}, one 15°, and one crystal in {Color A}. Skip one up bead and pass through the second "up" bead on the base. String on one crystal {Color B}, one 15° seed bead and one 4mm crystal {Color B}. Pass through the second "up" bead on the base. Repeat all the way around the base.

After you have completed adding the crystals on the first side weave your needle to the other side of the base. With the needle exiting an "up" bead in the base, making sure you are exactly opposite the "up" bead used on the first side, string on one crystal bicone in the same color as used on the other side. Pass through the 15° in the center of the two crystals previously attached on the opposite side. String another bicone and pass through the second 15° and continue adding bicones until all flowers are complete.

If you choose to use the 4mm bicones, you may need to retrace the thread paths several times in order to make the bicones lay properly on the base. The 3mm bicones usually do not need the additional thread but I would recommend it just because the crystals can be sharp and it is a little insurance policy for your finished beadwork.

When you have completed adding the crystals, work two more rows of peyote on each side of the circle. Tie off and bury the threads.

Gemstone and Pearls Circle

Supplies

15° galvanized gold seed beads, 1g

4 of the 5mm Gemstones

4 of the 2 to 3 mm freshwater pearls

Needle size 11 or 12

4lb test Fireline thread

Instructions

You can use some gemstones in the circles as well. The gemstones used in this example are about 5 - 6 mm in size, so the pearls used were very tiny. Follow the instructions for the cubes and pearls to use gemstones that are around 5mm in size. Gemstones that are flatter tend to work better.

The instruction for this Circle are the same as those for the cubes and pearls, but you will be substituting the gemstone beads for the cubes. The possibilities for the combinations are endless and you can customize them using a gemstone in a birthstone color to signify a child or grandchild, or perhaps some turquoise beads to represent a trip to the Southwest, jade for a trip to Japan or China, coral to represent a seaside vacation. Where did you spend your honeymoon – perhaps you can find a gemstone that holds a memory of that special time.

Make a 5 row peyote base. Weave your needle to the middle bead in one of the stacks of three. String on two 15°, one 5mm gemstone, two 15° seed bead. Skip the next middle bead and go through the second middle bead. Then string on one 15°, one pearl, one 15° and go through the second middle bead. Repeat around until you have four gemstones and four pearls.

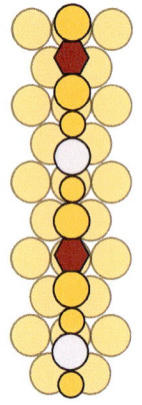

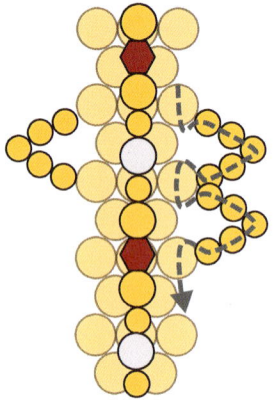

To embellish the sides use a 5 bead picot by exiting one of the "up" beads on one side of the circle. Pick up five 15° beads and go through the next "up" bead on that side. Repeat on the second side. Then connect the third bead of each picot together on the top of the circle.

✷ You could also use fire polished beads that are 5mm in size. The round ones work better than the bicone shape.

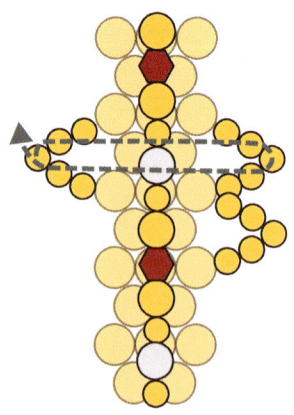

Anniversary Circle

Supplies

15° galvanized gold or silver seed beads, 1g

16 of the 2mm round crystals

Needle size 11 or 12

4lb test Fireline thread

Instructions

Make a 5 row peyote base. Using 2mm faceted round crystals, attach the crystal using the "up" beads on the peyote base. Follow the thread path to the right. You will come out of the edge bead, add the crystal go through the opposite edge bead and go back through the crystal and then through the first edge bead in the same direction. Pull the tension tight, but remember that crystals can cut the fireline so not too tight.

After you have attached the 16 crystals using all of the "up" beads, peyote around two more times on each edge, don't forget to step up at the end of the rounds. Notice that the "up" beads when pulled tight to the crystals are raised from their original position. This makes it possible to do the additional rows of peyote. This drawing shows only row one.

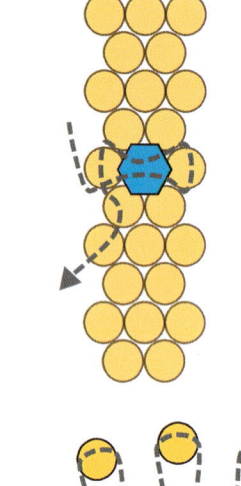

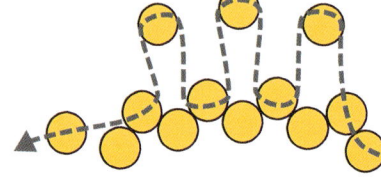

* When adding the two rows of peyote, pulling too tight could force the 15°s to lie back down. So, just pull tight enough to keep them in an upright positions

If the crystals still seem a little loose, go back through them until they feel tight. When you have completed the 2 rows on each side, go back through the crystals using the "up" beads from the last row on each side to pull the rows up snug with the crystals. Use the same thread path that you used when you first attached the crystals. Tie off and bury threads.

14

Double Anniversary Circle

Supplies

15° galvanized gold or silver seed beads, 2g

32 of the 2mm round crystals

Needle size 11 or 12

4lb test Fireline thread

Instructions

Make a 9 row peyote base. With your thread coming out of an "up" bead on the edge of the circle, string on a set of one 2mm faceted round crystal, a 15° seed bead and a 2mm round crystal. Attach the set to the "up" bead on the opposite edge of the peyote circle base. Follow the thread path to the right. Go back through the set of crystals in the opposite direction and go through the first edge bead in the same direction as you originally used. Make sure to pull the tension tight, but remember that crystals can cut the fireline so not too tight.

After you have attached the 16 crystal sets using all of the "up" beads, peyote around two more times on each side. Don't forget to step up at the end of the rounds. Notice that the "up" beads when pulled tight to the crystals are raised from their original position. This makes it possible to do the additional rows of peyote. This drawing shows only row one. Don't pull the tension too tight or these rows won't lie correctly. If the tension is too tight, the beads will not sit upright.

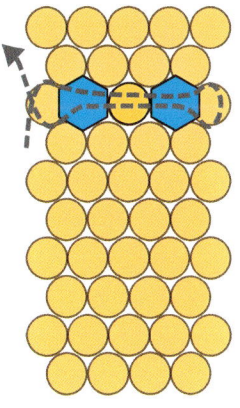

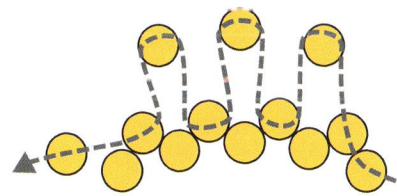

If the crystals still seem a little loose, go back through them until they feel tight. When you have completed the 2 rows on each side, go back through the crystals using the "up" beads from the last row on each side to pull the rows up snug with the crystal sets. Use the same thread path that you used when you first attached the crystals. Tie off and bury the threads.

Heart Circle

Supplies

15° galvanized gold or silver seed beads, 1g

8 of the 5mm heart shaped beads with a vertical hole

Needle size 11 or 12

4 lb test Fireline thread

Instructions

The small heart circle begins with a five row peyote base. Exiting through the bottom of one of the center 15° beads, pick up a 15°, a heart and another 15° bead. Attach the set of beads to the base going through the center bead in the second row of three beads.

Go back up through the last 15° from the previous step and pick up a heart and one 15° bead and go through the center bead of the second row of three beads on the base. See diagram.

Embellish the circles by exiting one of the 15° beads between the hearts pointing in the same direction, picking up as many beads as needed to smoothly reach the second "up" bead on the edge from the row where you began. Each of the outlines around the hearts will overlap slightly to create an interesting edge effect. Repeat on the second side. Tie off and bury the threads.

16

Single Rope Spacer Circle

Supplies

15° galvanized gold and silver seed beads, 1.25g

Needle size 11 or 12

4lb test Fireline thread

Instructions

Begin with a five row base. With the fireline exiting from one of the "up" beads in the base, string on seven size 15° beads and go through the "up" bead on the opposite side that is the third "up" from the place you began. Go through the bead heading back toward the opposite side and go straight through the five beads that are diagonally lined up. Repeat sixteen times around to cover the entire base. Tie off and bury the threads.

For a variation use two colors for the "ropes" alternating each one.

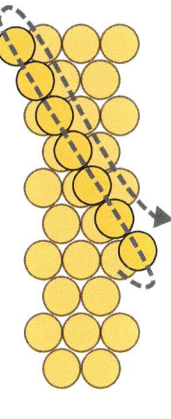

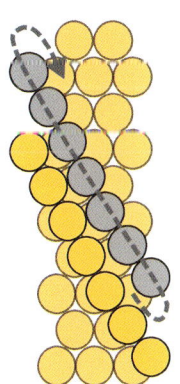

17

Crystal Rope Circle

Supplies

15° galvanized gold seed beads, 1g

16 of the 3mm round crystals or firepolish

32 of the 2mm round crystals

Needle size 11 or 12

4lb test Fireline thread

Instructions

Start off the circle with a five row base. The embellishment is exactly the same method as the rope spacer, except that this time you will use three 15°, one 2mm round crystal, one 3mm round crystal, one 2mm round crystal, and three 15° beads. Place the set of beads diagonally across the base and use the third up bead on the opposite side. Go back diagonally through the beads and repeat the process all the way around. You will need sixteen diagonal sets. Tie off and bury the threads.

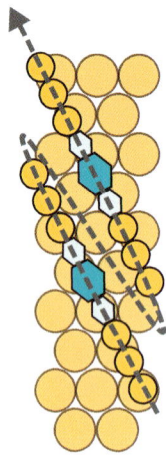

Double Rope Spacer

Supplies

15° galvanized gold and silver seed beads, 2g

Needle size 11 or 12

4lb test Fireline thread

Instructions

Begin with a nine row base. Just as for the single rope, with the thread exiting from one of the "up" beads, string on seven size 15° and go through the center bead three center beads up from the starting point. Then go directly through the diagonal beads and exit from the "up" that is above the one you started with. Repeat sixteen times to cover one side. Then turn your work around. Repeat on the second side as shown below in the diagram. You will need to work sixteen ropes on the other side as well. You could also dress up the rope bead by adding crystals around the center of the double rope bead. Tie off and bury the threads.

As with the single rope spacer bead you could use two colors and alternate them.

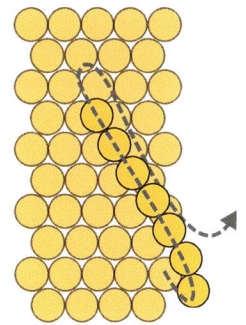

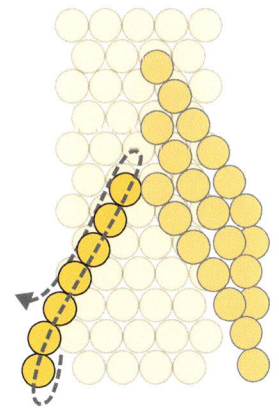

19

Seed Bead Spacer

Supplies

15° galvanized gold seed beads, 1.5g

11° colored seed beads, .5g

Needle size 11 or 12

4lb test Fireline thread

Instructions

Begin with an eleven row base using 15° beads.

The base is embellished in layers. For the first layer, with the thread coming out of a "down" bead on the edge of the base, string on one 15° in the same color as the base. Go through the next "down" bead on the edge of the base. Repeat around the base. For the second row of the layer use the middle bead of the "down" bead row and add a 15° between each of the middle beads in the "down" bead row. For the third row of this layer, repeat the first row on the other edge of the base.

For the second layer, with the thread coming out of one of the ffirst layer's edge bead, pick up an 11° bead and go through the center row from the previous layer following the thread path as shown in the diagram. The thread path depicted is right angle weave (RAW). Repeat around the base until you have added two rows. Tie off and bury the threads.

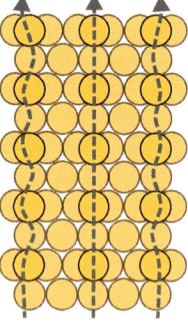

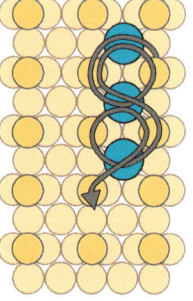

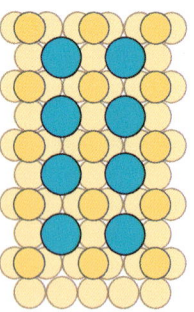

*If you wish to embellish the bead further you can add a third layer utilizing RAW as shown in the diagram.

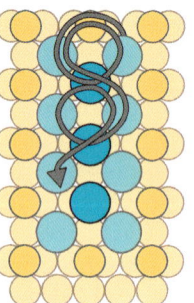

Netted Crystal Circle

Supplies

15° galvanized gold seed beads, 1.5g

15° galvanized silver seed beads, .3g

24 of the 3mm round crystals

Needle size 11 or 12

4lb test Fireline thread

Instructions

Start with an eleven row base. Work the netting as follows: With the thread coming out of a "up" bead on the edge of the base, Sting on seven 15° beads and go through the second "up" bead on the edge (skipping over one "up" bead. You will be stringing on seven beads and using every other up bead on the edge.

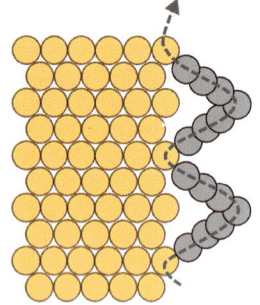

For the second row of netting, weave the needle to the center of the first seven beads in the prior row. You will be coming out of the fourth bead. String on seven bead and go through the middle bead in the next set of seven beads. Work this all the way around.

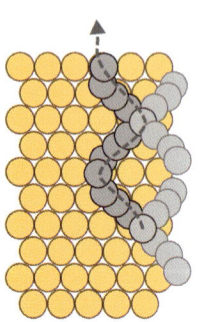

For the third row of netting, weave the needle to the center of the first seven beads in the prior row. You will be coming out of the fourth bead. String on seven bead and go through the middle bead in the next set of seven beads. Work this all the way around.

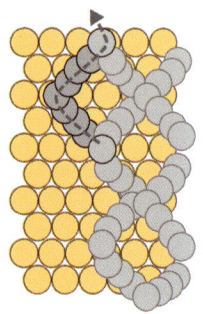

For the final netting row, weave your needle to the center of the seven bead group from the previous row. String on three beads, go through the "up" bead on the far edge of the base. Make sure that this bead corresponds to the one used for the first row of netting.

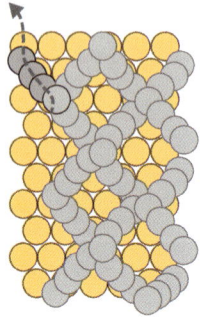

22

Go through that edge bead, string on three beads, go through the center bead in the group of seven beads from the previous row of netting. Work in this same manner all the way around.

After the netting is completed, go back through the thread path a few times to make the netting firmer. Then with your needle exiting one of the middle beads in the last row of netting, add one 4mm round crystal and go through the shared bead in the next set.

Add three rows of crystals utilizing each diamond shape in the netting around the circle.

You may want to retrace the thread path to tighten up the tension and also as an extra protection since the crystals can sometimes cut the fireline. Tie off and bury the threads.

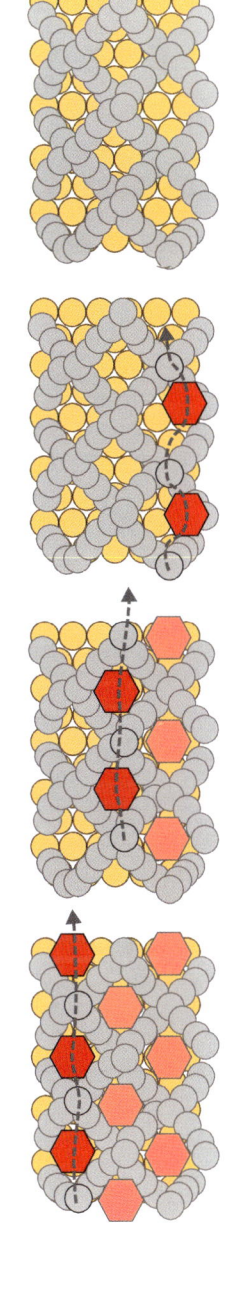

Netted Overlay Circle

Supplies

15° galvanized gold seed beads, 1.25g

15° galvanized silver seed beads, .75g

Needle size 11 or 12

4lb test Fireline thread

Instructions

Begin with a nine row base. With the thread exiting an "up" bead on the edge of the base, sting on nine beads and go through the second "up" bead. You will be using every other "up bead on the edge of the base. Repeat around the base. Then weave your needle to the other edge of the base, being careful to use the "up" that is directly across the base from the "up" bead used on the first edge, string on four beads, got through the middle bead of the set of nine bead attached to the first edge of the base, then string on four more beads and go through the second "up" bead making sure that it matches with the "up" bead used on the other edge of the base. You may wish to retrace the thread path for the netting in order to firm it up if it is a little loose. Tie off and bury the threads.

*You could embellish further by stitching beads into the spaces made by the nets.

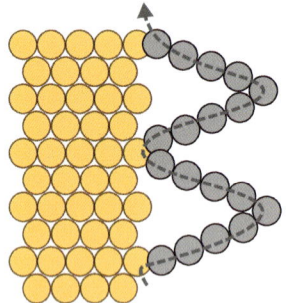

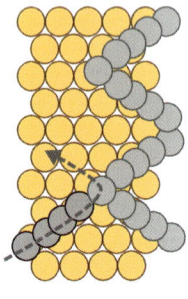

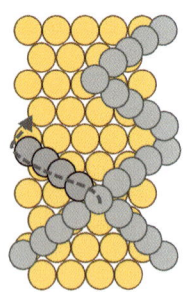

24

The Charm Spacer Circle

Supplies

15° galvanized gold or silver seed beads, .5g

11° galvanized gold or silver seed beads, 1g

Needle size 11 or 12

4lb test Fireline thread

Instructions

The charm spacer begins with a three row base.

Row 4: peyote around alternating size 11° beads and size 15° beads.

Row 5: peyote around using size 11° beads.

Row 6: Peyote around using size 11° beads.

Weave the thread to the other side of the three row base. Repeat rows 4 and 5.

"Zip" the size 11° beads together to form a ring.

You can add crystals to the outer edge of the ring by stitching in the ditch between the beads of row 6. We used 2.5 mm crystals. If you are adding a charm, only place 14 crystals around. Then with the needle exiting the center next outside edge bead in row 6, add 7 to 9 size 15° beads and form a loop to attach the charm. You will want to adjust your loop to make sure that it can accommodate the charm of your choice and you may want to orient your loop based on the orientation of your charm.

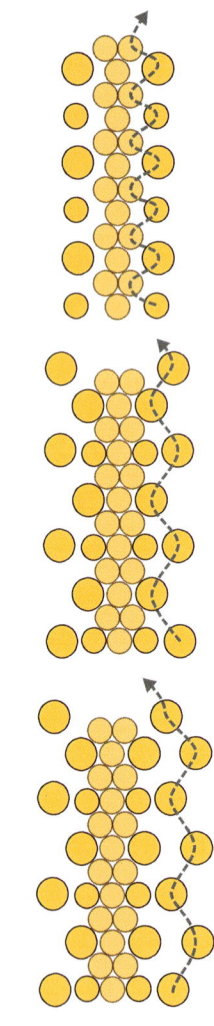
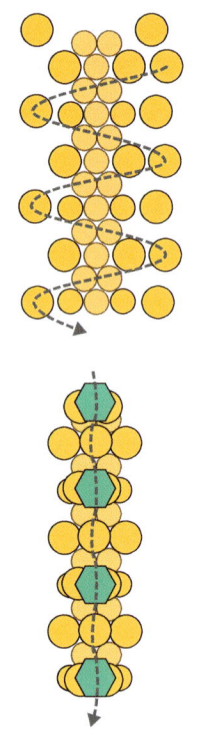

*This works with size 11 delica beads versus size 11 seed beads also.

The Heart Charm

Supplies

15° galvanized silver seed beads, 1g

63 of the 3mm bicone swarovski crystals

Needle size 11 or 12

4lb test Fireline thread

Instructions

Thread a needle with about 1-½ yards of thread or fireline. String on a seed bead, a crystal, a seed bead, a crystal, a seed bead and a crystal. Tie beads into a circle leaving a 6 inch tail to be woven in later.

Weave the thread so that it is exiting one of the crystals. String on a seed bead, a crystal, a seed bead, a crystal and a seed bead. Go back through the crystal that the thread is coming out of. You will be going in a circle.

Weave the thread so that it is exiting one of the crystals. String on a seed bead, a crystal, a seed bead, a crystal and a seed bead. Go back through the crystal that the thread is coming out of. You will be going in a circle. Notice that this time you will be going in the opposite direction.

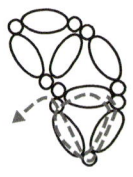

Continuing in the circle of beads just added, weave the thread back through a seed bead, a crystal, a seed bead, a crystal so that it is exiting a crystal. String on a seed bead, a crystal, a seed bead, a crystal and a seed bead. Go back through the crystal that the thread is coming out of. You will be going in a circle.

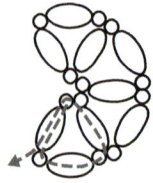

Continuing in the circle of beads just added, weave the thread back through a seed bead and a crystal. String on a seed bead, a crystal, a seed bead, a crystal, and a seed bead. Go back through the crystal that the thread is coming out of. You will be going in a circle. Notice that this time you will be going in the opposite direction.

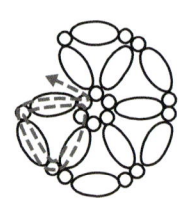

Continuing in the circle of beads just added, weave the thread back through a seed bead, a crystal, a seed bead, a crystal so that it is exiting a crystal. To complete the circle, pick up a seed bead and go through the crystal of the first triangle. Pick up a seed bead, a crystal, and a seed bead. Go through the crystal from the last triangle. Weave the thread through the circle of seeds at the center to pull them tight.

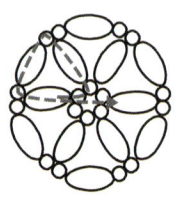

The heart is composed of five circles like this one, but they overlap each other. The next circle you will stitch will use the beads that are colored in this diagram. Weave your thread so that it is exiting the circle as shown below. There are six "spoke" beads in each circle and six outside beads in each circle. When I refer to a "spoke" bead, that will be the one that points to the center of the circle.

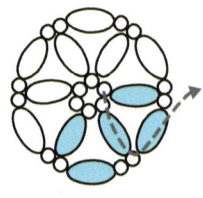

I am not going to draw every thread path now because it is basically the same for each of the circles. Always make sure that your needle is coming out of a "spoke" bead before picking up the beads for the next step.

Pick up one seed bead, one crystal, one seed bead, one crystal and one seed bead. Go back through the crystal that the thread is coming out of. Weave back through the beads just added until the thread is coming out of the "spoke" bead by going through 1 seed bead, 1 crystal, 1 seed bead and 1 crystal.

Pick up one seed bead, one crystal, one seed bead, one crystal and one seed bead. Go back through the crystal that the thread is coming out of. Weave back through the beads just added until the thread is coming out of the "spoke" bead.

Pick up one seed bead, one crystal, one seed bead, one crystal and one seed bead. Go back through the crystal that the thread is coming out of. Weave back through the beads just added until the thread is coming out of the "spoke" bead.

Pick up a seed bead and go through the first "spoke" bead in the circle. Pick up a seed bead, a crystal and a seed bead and go through the last spoke bead in the circle. Reenforce the center of this circle by weaving through all of the center seed beads once again.

The next circle is formed using the highlighted beads from the second circle. See Diagram. Weave through the second circle so you are exiting the crystal shown here in this diagram.

Pick up one seed bead, one crystal, one seed bead, one crystal and one seed bead. Go back through the crystal that the thread is coming out of. Weave back through the beads just added until the thread is coming out of the "spoke" bead by going through 1 seed bead, 1 crystal, 1 seed bead and 1 crystal.

Pick up one seed bead, one crystal, one seed bead, one crystal and one seed bead. Go back through the crystal that the thread is coming out of. Weave back through the beads just added until the thread is coming out of the "spoke" bead.

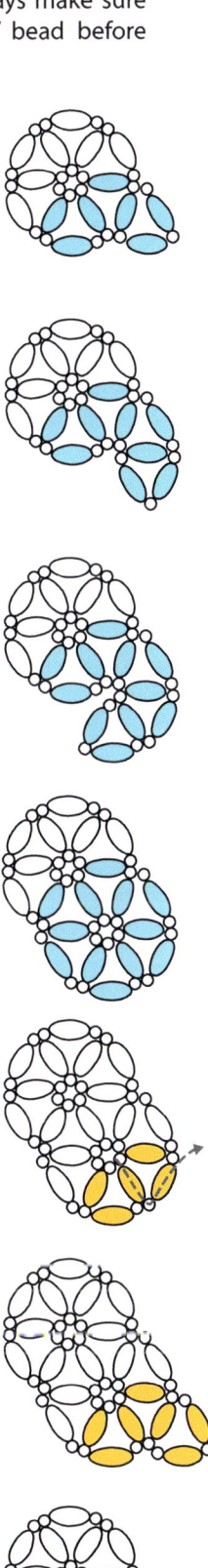

29

Pick up one seed bead, one crystal, one seed bead, one crystal and one seed bead. Go back through the crystal that the thread is coming out of. Weave back through the beads just added until the thread is coming out of the "spoke" bead.

Pick up a seed bead and go through the last "spoke" bead in the circle. Pick up a seed bead, a crystal and a seed bead and go through the first "spoke" bead in the circle Weave your thread to the center of the circle and go through the six seed beads to tighten them up.

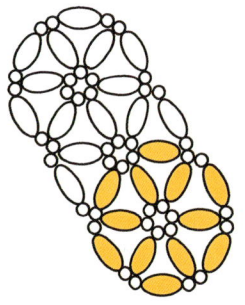

The fourth circle of the heart will be made with the highlighted beads shown in the diagram to the right. Weave your thread so that it is exiting the bead as shown in the diagram.

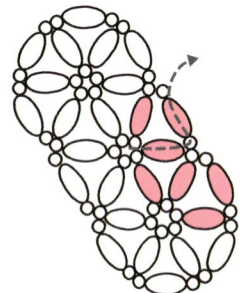

Pick up a seed bead, a crystal, a seed bead, a crystal and a seed bead. Go back through the bead that the thread is coming out of. Weave the thread through until it is coming out of the "'spoke' bead" just added.

Pick up a seed bead, a crystal, a seed bead, a crystal and a seed bead. Go back through the bead that the thread is exiting. Weave through until your thread is coming out of a "'spoke' bead."

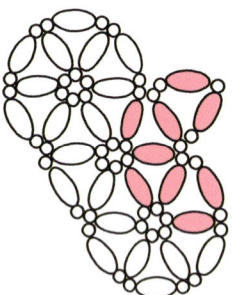

Pick up a seed bead, a crystal and a seed bead. Go through the first "spoke" bead in the circle, pick up a seed bead and go through the last "spoke" bead in the circle. Weave the thread to the center of the circle and go through all of the seed beads to tighten up.

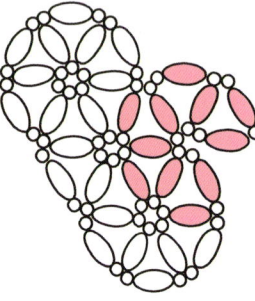

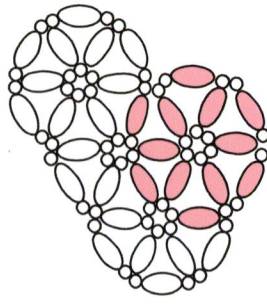

Now for the last circle. You will use the beads that are highlighted in green to complete the last circle of the heart. Weave your thread so that it is coming out of the bead shown in the diagram.

Pick up a seed bead, a crystal, a seed bead, a crystal and a seed bead. Go back through the bead that the thread is coming out of. Weave the thread through until it is coming out of the "spoke bead" just added. Pick up one seed bead, one crystal, one seed bead, one crystal and one seed bead. Go back through the crystal that the thread is coming out of. Weave back through the beads just added until the thread is coming out of the "spoke" bead.

Pick up a seed bead and go through the last "spoke" bead in the circle. Pick up a seed bead, a crystal and a seed bead and go through the first "spoke" bead in the circle Weave your thread to the center of the circle and go through the six seed beads to tighten them up.

The fourth circle of the heart will be made with the highlighted beads shown in the diagram to the right. Weave your thread so that it is exiting the bead as shown in this diagram that is shown on the right.

Pick up a seed bead, a crystal, a seed bead, a crystal and a seed bead. Go back through the bead that the thread is coming out of. Weave the thread through until it is coming out of the ""spoke" bead" just added.

Pick up a seed bead and go through the last "spoke bead" in the circle. Pick up a seed bead, a crystal and a seed bead. Go through the first "spoke bead" in the circle. Weave the thread to the center of the circle and go through all of the seed beads to tighten up.

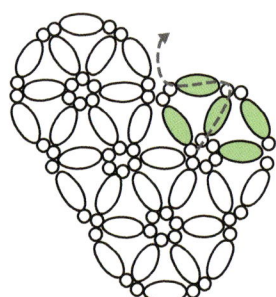

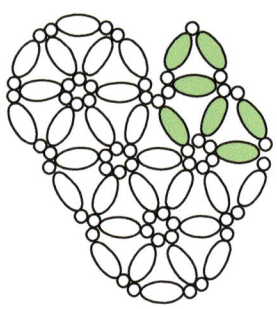

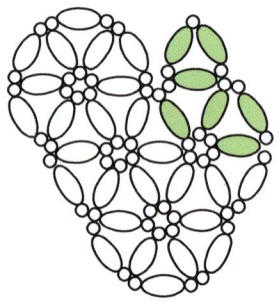

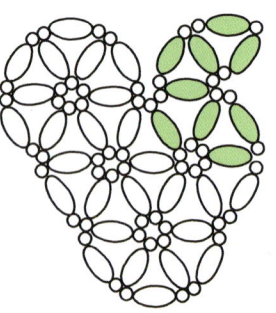

30

Now that you have finished the first side of the heart, we will proceed to the back side. The two sides share the outside beads of the heart. The shared beads are shaded in this diagram. Weave your thread so that it is exiting the outside bead as shown (remember to flip your heart over so that you only have to weave through a few beads.)

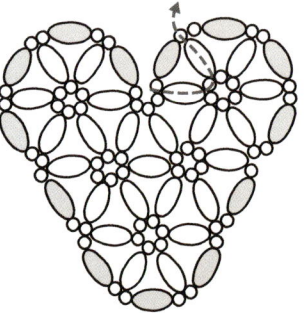

Pick up a seed bead, a crystal, a seed bead, a crystal and a seed bead. Go back through the outside bead and weave through the first seed bead and first crystal added.

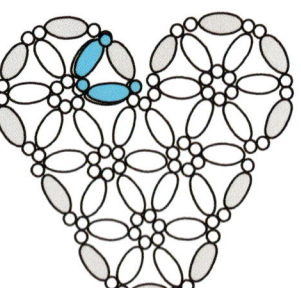

Pick up one seed bead, one crystal and one seed bead, go through the shared bead, pick up one seed bead and go through the "spoke" bead from the last step. Weave your needle through to the "spoke" bead added in this step.

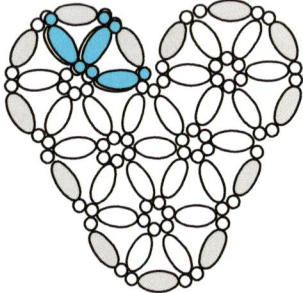

Pick up one seed bead and go through the shared bead, pick up one seed bead, one crystal and one seed bead and go through the "spoke" bead from the last step. Weave your needle through to the "spoke" bead added in this step.

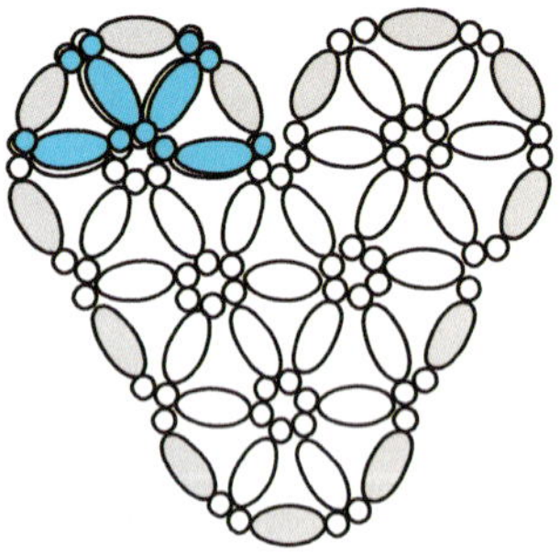

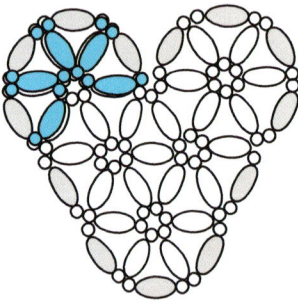

Pick up one seed bead, one crystal and one seed bead, go through the shared bead, pick up one seed bead and go through the "spoke" bead from the last step. Weave your needle through to the "spoke" bead added in this step.

Pick up one seed bead, one crystal and one seed bead, one crystal (notice that there is no shared bead in this step), pick up one seed bead and go through the "spoke" bead from the last step. Weave your needle through to the "spoke" bead added in this step.

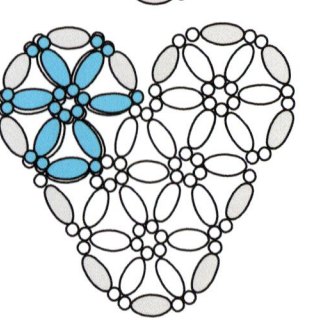

Pick up one seed bead and go back through the first "spoke" bead of the circle you are finishing. Pick up one seed bead, one crystal, one seed bead, go through the "spoke" bead added in this step.

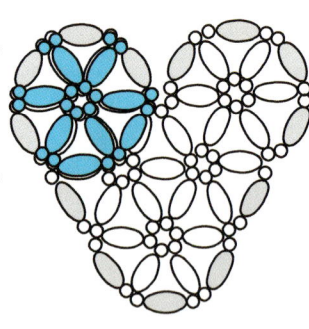

So you get the idea now, where there is a shared bead you substitute the shared bead for a crystal and where there is not a shared bead it is stitching as usual.

When the second side of the heart in complete go around the edges and go through the seed beads to tighten them up. This will help your heart to hold its shape. If you look at the edge of your heart, you will see a cluster of 4 or 6 seed beads in between each crystal. Sew around the heart, through each crystal and around each cluster of beads.

When you get to the V of the heart, you will see 5 seed bead on each side of the heart. Add one seed bead at the top and sew through the group of 6 seed beads in a circle. Flip your heart and sew around the circle from the other side. When the circles are nice and tight, you can add a loop of seed beads in order to create a bail. We used 12 seed beads and went back through them several times to create strength at the stress point.

These hearts can be made from any combination of beads. The pictures below show hearts made from semi-precious gemstone beads and seed beads. Change the size of the seed beads as the size of the gemstone decreases.

The Starfish Charm

Supplies

15° galvanized gold seed beads, 1g

15° galvanized silver seed beads, 1g

Small piece of foam

Needle size 11 or 12

4lb test Fireline thread

Instructions

In these instructions the gold 15° seed beads will be referred to as {Color A} and the silver as {Color B}.

Pick up 5 size 15° seed beads in {Color A}. Tie them into a circle.

Place a single bead in between each of the beads in the previous row. Step up at the end of this row and each row after.

Place two {Color A} beads in between each of the beads in the previous row.

Place two {Color A} beads on top of the pairs from the previous row and a single {Color B} bead in between the pairs from the previous row.

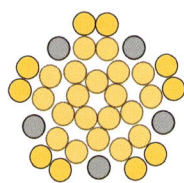

Place two {Color A} beads on top of the pairs and peyote two single {Color B} beads between.

34

Place double {Color A} beads on top of the pairs from the previous row and peyote one single {Color B} bead go throught the next bead without a bead on the needle (decrease), then one single {Color B} bead. Place pairs on top of the pairs using {Color A} then three single peyote with {Color B} between the pairs.

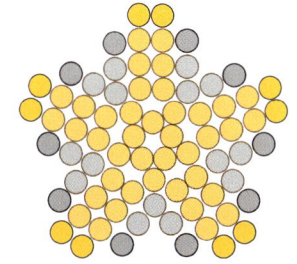

Place pairs on top of the pairs using {Color A}, then three single peyote with {Color B} between the pairs.

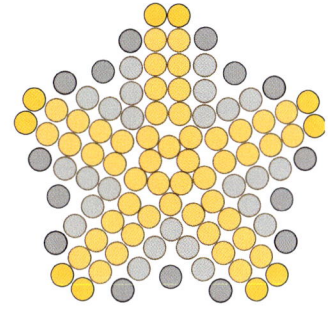

Place pairs on top of the pairs using {Color A}, then single peyote with {Color B} between the pairs.

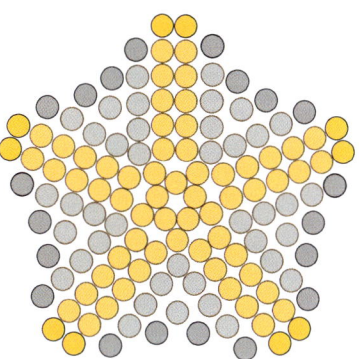

Place pairs on top of the pairs using {Color A}, then single peyote with {Color B} for two stitches, then go throught the next bead without a bead on the needle (decrease), then peyote two single stitches with {Color B}.

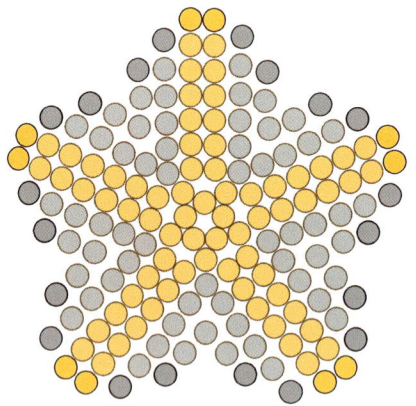

Place pairs on top of the pairs using {Color A}, then single peyote with {Color B} between the pairs.

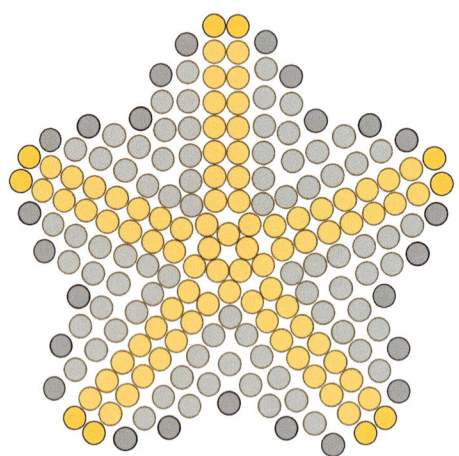

Place a single {Color A} on top of the pairs and single {Color B} peyote in between.

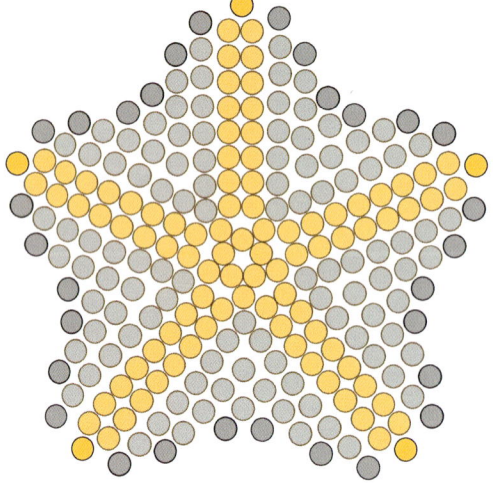

Make a second side exactly like the first side but do not use row 11. After Row 10 of the second side, begin zipping the two sides together. You may wish to stuff the center with either plastic grocery bags cut into small strips or a small piece of foam or even bathroom tissue will work. This will keep the starfish puffed out.

Twisted Herringbone Rope

Supplies

15° galvanized gold seed beads, 9g

15° galvanized silver seed beads, 9g

Magnetic Clasp

Needle size 11 or 12

4lb test Fireline thread

Instructions

Make a twisted vine using 15° beads in the two colors. Alternate each color. Begin with a two bead ladder that is six beads long. Form into a circle attaching the row to the first.

To make the herringbone spiral you will pick up two beads, one bead of each color, go down one bead and up two beads. Repeat. On the third time, go down one bead and up three beads, doing a "step up" at the end of the row. Of course yours will be in a circle, but these diagrams will be flat.

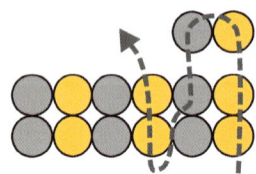

For the third and susequent rows, you will pick up one bead of each color, and go down one bead of the next stack and up three beads in the following stack.

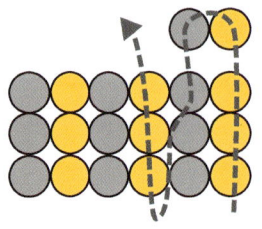

For the remainder of the herringbone spiral you will always go down one bead after adding the two new beads and come up through three beads in the next stack. The tube will begin to twist but you may not see it until about ½ inch of stitching. Note that there is no need to worry about a "step up."

For the last three rows of the necklace, do one row by picking up two beads each time, going down one bead and up two, down one bead and up two, and down one bead and up three.

The last two rows, pick up two beads, go down one bead and up one, down one bead and up one, down one bead and up two.

For a final step, ladder stitch the last two rows together by weaving in the opposite direction without picking up beads going down two beads and up two beads around the circle. This makes the two ends of your necklace look alike.

This size of necklace will accommodate easily any of the Circle Beads that you make from these directions. Sitich the length to your choice but remember that because the circle beads are wide they will take up space on the rope. You may wait to make the closure until you have your circles complete so you can adjust the length of the rope. Because of the way that the closure is constructed, you will be able to add and remove any of the circle beads to change up your look or to represent an additional event in your life.

Resources

Flat Peyote Stitch Instructions

If you do not know how to do peyote stitch you may want to practice flat even-count peyote prior to attempting the tubular peyote used in the bases for the Circles of Life.

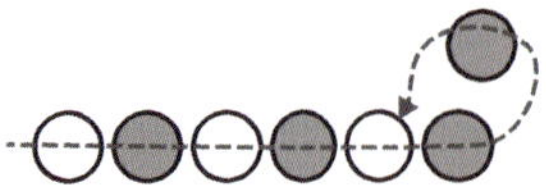

It is helpful to use two colors of beads while you are learning.

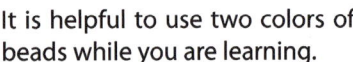

String on alternating colors so that you have an even number of beads. I am using six beads in the diagrams. Then pick up a grey bead, skip over the last grey bead and go through the white bead. You will be actually stitching the third row. The first beads that were strung on make up the first and second rows. This becomes more obvious after the third row is complete.

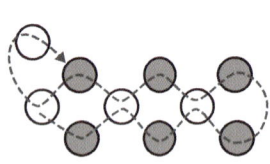

At the end of the third row you will turn around and head back in the other direction. Pick up a white bead and go through the next grey bead. You will only be adding white beads on this row.

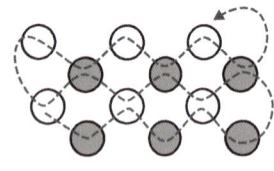

For the next row repeat with grey beads going back in the other direction.

Tubular Peyote Stitch Instructions

The only difference between flat even count peyote and tubular peyote is that the flat strip will be made into a circle.

Begin with an even number of beads and tie them into a circle. With the thread exiting from a grey bead, pick up a white bead and stitch through the next grey bead. Repeat all the way around. The big difference is that you will need to "step up" to start the next round. That means that you will need to pass the needle through the first bead added in this round. When you stitch pull the thread tension tight and it will form a cigar band shape.

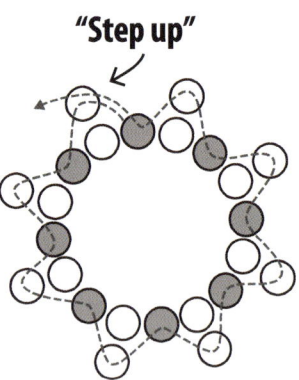

You may also want to consider beading around a tube shaped object such as a pen or a wooden dowel to make it easier.

Surgeon's Knot

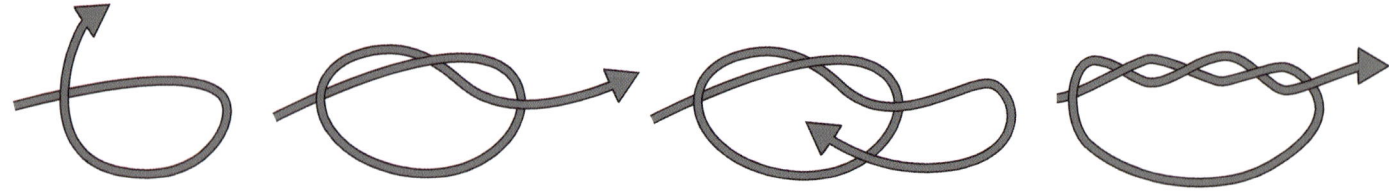

40

Netting Stitch Instructions

The basic flat netting stitch is shown in the diagrams. Begin by stinging on one {Color A} and two {Color B} repeating until the net is the desired length. The for the turnaround at the bottom, string on three additional {Color B} beads, one {Color A}, two {Color B} and then go through the color a bead from the first row as shown in the diagram. As you can see a "net" beginning to form.

Again the only difference with the netting used in the Circles of life is that there is not a turnaround. Rather you will complete the net in a circle around the bead. Then you will continue for additional rows around the circle until the desired width is achieved.

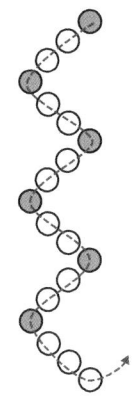
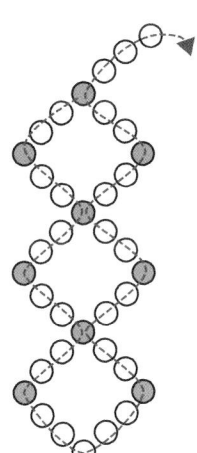

Herringbone Stitch Instructions

This is an alternative method of starting the stitch without using a ladder stitch to begin. Start by picking up twelve beads. The first bead will be white and then you will follow the pattern of alternating double grey and double white. At the end of the twelve though you will end on one white just like you began.

To begin the stitch add a bead to make the turn, in this case I used a grey bead. Coming out of the white bead string on the grey bead and pass back through the white bead. You will then skip the next two grey beads and pass through the other next white bead.

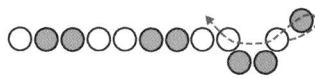

You will then add on two more grey beads and pass through the next white bead. This stitch will create an interesting appearance, that is emphasized more when using tubular shaped beads. Repeat these steps all the way down the row.

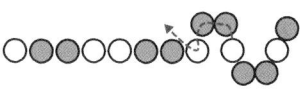

To turn add on one grey bead and a white bead and pass back through the grey bead that you just added and then skip the next two white beads passing back through the next grey bead. Continue to use this method until you have reached your desired length. Tie off and bury the thread. The only difference between flat herringbone and tubular is that in tubular you are working in a complete circle.

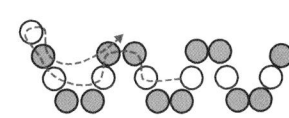

Square Knot

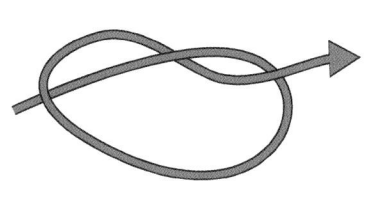
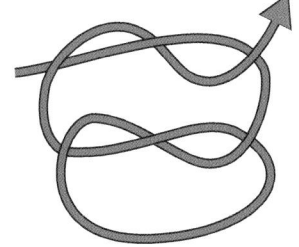
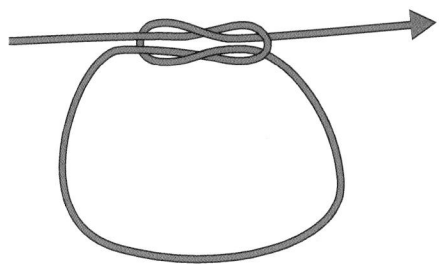

Elizabeth Townes
BeadJewled, Inc.
www.beadjeweledinc.com

Printed in Great Britain
by Amazon.co.uk, Ltd.,
Marston Gate.